T0286346

HOME REMEMBERS ME

HOME REMEMBERS ME

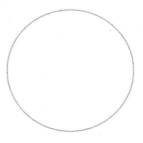

Medicine Poems from
em claire

Home Remembers Me

Em Claire

Copyright © 2013 by Em Claire
All rights reserved, including the right to reproduce this
work in any form whatsoever, without permission
in writing from the publisher, except for brief passages
in connection with a review.

Cover and interior design by Frame25 Productions

EmNin Books
PO Box 1085
Ashland, OR 97520
silvergirloffice@gmail.com

Distributed by:
Hay House, Inc.
P.O. Box 5100
Carlsbad, CA 92018-5100
www.hayhouse.com

Library of Congress Cataloging-in-Publication Data
available upon request.

ISBN 978-1-4019-4445-2

10 9 8 7 6 5 4 3 2 1

Printed on acid-free paper in Canada

For Neale,

my Beloved Other and Soul Companion,

in more ways than there are lifetimes . . .

I'll see you in the next one, My Love—

Your Forever *em*

INTRODUCTION

I imagine that my life has been similar to most people's lives: times of profound happiness and times of profound grief. A few fantastic achievements, and a number of fantastic failures. I have loved and lost family, friends, relationships, beloved animals and faith in cherished ideas and ideals.

There have been chapters of deep devotion, connection and awareness, and chapters of flagrant disregard. I have known physical, mental, and emotional pain that I thought would never leave, and I have known comfort, contentment and grace that I thought would always remain.

And there have been moments of profound intimacy with life—as well as loneliness so lonesome that I was certain I was nothing more than a particle of dust, floating through the universe and with no Home, *anywhere* in it…

But I've come to know that we are Spirit, exploring how to walk on the wobbly legs of a very young species: the Human, *Being*—with all of its tenderness and beauty, as well as its shadows and hidden compartments, and complexities so complex that they can surprise even the most committed seeker of Universal

Truths. Yet *as* Spirit, we are made of Goodness, and our lives are sacred and worthwhile, and we are each loved and supported and treasured—more profoundly than we could ever imagine.

You are made of Goodness. And your life is sacred, and worthwhile, and you are loved and supported and cherished—more profoundly than you could ever imagine.

No matter what we are currently experiencing, I believe that it is exactly right *for the sake of the Soul,* and that we are adding our unique strand of light to an eternal tapestry that's being woven—all in the name of Love. All in the name of the Intelligent Presence that lives through us, *as us,* as It celebrates our every question, our every yearning, our every so-called stumble and brilliant revelation. I think, as my husband is fond of saying, that we are indeed God, *Godding...* How else would Divinity come to experience Itself but through us, and through all forms of life? Given this, is there really a way to do it "wrong"?

Tell that to a Tree and it will tell you that it's just *Tree*-ing, and wherever its seed innocently took root, no matter the quality of the soil or the kind of environment it began in: the open space or the cramped conditions; the consistent climate or the unpredictable storms; the broad light of an open sky or the dim shadows of a crowded canopy—it's just Tree-ing. And it knows that it has been given everything it needs in order to just keep on *growing toward the sun.*

Everything it needs to just *keep on growing*—
because the work of the Soul
is never done. Life is never done.
God is never done.

Love is never done.

○

And this is where *You* come in.

The continuing expansion of soul can often create extremes, and within the experience of humanity in the times we're living in, I believe our collective soul has embarked on an individual and a communal *Medicine Walk*.

For the sake of humanity and the planet and all of its life forms; for the sake of this breathing, living universe we are alive in and a part of and affecting with our thoughts, words and actions, we are each being called to discover our *individual purpose and gifts*, that we might bring them back to the Tribe—a species that is deeply out-of-balance and that is deeply wounded and struggling.

In certain Native American cultures a *medicine walk* was taken when it was time to find one's personal medicine, which in the Native American sense was anything that was healing and positive to the body and mind, and which encouraged and supported living in harmony with one's self, with the tribe and with the planet.

Similar to a *vision quest*, in *medicine walks* the ones seeking answers were supported in leaving the tribe for a time to spend days in the wilderness, where they would fast and listen and observe. They paid silent attention to the weather, animals, and landscapes, to help them interpret their own life and understand their individual purpose, seeking wisdom and guidance in nature by looking for symbolic meaning from the things they witnessed and perceived.

The "messages" they received not only helped them to know their purpose in life, but also revealed their special gifts and talents, and instructed them as to how to use those gifts to benefit their tribe when they returned.

The yearning to find your personal medicine may be brought on through illness, divorce, financial loss, or sudden homelessness, addictions or the recovery process…even the death of a loved one who has chosen to gift you with the fierce grace of a space with which to now discover your *next* Calling, bringing yet greater medicine to the deeply struggling larger family.

Or you may find yourself drawn to make a sudden choice to stop everything—to slow down, carve out a few sacred days or months and literally take a walk in the woods, or sit at the ocean's edge, *listening*. Maybe even listening and observing the natural world for the very first time.

A wonderful woman who devotes her life to helping people do just that, describes it this way:

"Medicine walks can be undertaken in preparation for important transitions in life…the insights you receive from a medicine walk can be subtle or immensely profound, and sometimes the answers aren't what you were expecting. But simply by embarking on a medicine walk, you invite a more mystical quality into your life. You acknowledge that the world is more than a collection of profane objects, but rather a world alive with both meaning and mystery."

—Margaret Emerson, *Contemplative Hiking Along the Colorado Front Range*

Our Tribe needs You now, more than ever before, to find your personal Medicine, and then to share it with every form of life you touch. When we do this we are saying, "Thank you. I acknowledge the gift I've been given. *The Gift of Me.* I will no longer play small. I will step fully into Who I AM, without apology, or self-consciousness, but in total awareness of the Goodness and the Grace and the Compassion and the Mercy and the Love I AM. My world needs Me and I'm no longer willing to ignore my individual purpose and the unique gifts that I came here to bring. I am Love, *Loving."*

○

Reflected in these poems is my own Medicine Walk. May they support you in finding or recovering or discovering the courage you will need to live your truth. May these poems be good medicine that Life is offering you, serving to nourish and support your body, mind, and spirit through the times in which we are living.

Throughout the poetry the word "God" appears often, but I invite you to mentally insert any word or name that fits your belief system and speaks to your soul. Whatever the image or idea, I hope that it is one that represents the kindest, gentlest source of goodness and tenderness and humor and friendship and support one could imagine.

These poems found you, and this is no accident. Know that you are Seen. Know that you are Heard. Know that you are Loved. Know that the god in which you believe has heard you, and recognizes the longing and the truth of your heart. And know that your Soul Tribe is gathering, and connected, heart-to-heart across the planet—and that you now have Family *everywhere*.

em claire
Ashland, Oregon
May 2013

I know that these words may open you

shamelessly.

For the surprise element I apologize.

But not for the response.

Never

for what it is that will be exposed to the Light.

There is that second before a second,

just before you cover and run,

when you hear the lightning of Truth

crackling through your skies

to find you again,

because Life wants you back.

I know that these words may open you—

shamelessly.

LONG AT SEA

I left Home so long ago now
that I would not recognize my own face.
I constructed the Boat of my Life
and I set out
into the open sea,
waving to all who knew
that the seas would give me
everything I could handle,
and everything I could not—
and yet they waved, and I set out
into the open sea
in the Boat of My Life:
built from Soul, crafted by Heart.
And with great innocence I pushed off
into the open sea
and have been away from my Home
so long now that I would not recognize my own face—
but I know that Home,

Home

remembers me.

ACRES AND ACRES

I see clearly now that there is always
so much space
to be Free in.

Who I thought was fencing me in
could have been
no one else
but Me!

I see
the blue and the white skies
like feathers for new wings;
like wings for my eyes . . .

The Human Being was about
to give up.

Oh, just before flight.
Oh, just before walking
out of the Night into
acres and acres
of
Light

LIFE IS MOSTLY QUIET

Believe me, you don't have to know.
Not so much that you render yourself helpless.
Helpless in the face of what Life brings next.
So make peace with knowing very little.
About Love.
About Others.
About how life *should* be.
Make amends with how things are.
Not knowing a thing,
walk with gentle knees,
ready to drop to them at any moment
that Life dictates.
Keep an empty hand
so that it can be brought to your heart
when a grief arrives.
Make up a bed that you can fall into
as your own comforting arms.

We come to find that Life is mostly quiet—
it asks us to *live by our Knowing,*
while surrendering that very same thing.
It vibrates easily around us,
candid and benevolent.
You see, it's only
when we root ourselves
solid in some Knowing again,
that Life seems to have to shout—
rises,
lovingly,
from Its whisper.

WHATEVER IT WAS

It is your own life that you desire to cherish

like one brings the downy tuft of a Dandelion to the lips

blows softly

prays

to give everything away

keep

only what remains

of a life well lived

a life well loved

nourished and blessed

by the suns and by the soils

and by whatever it was

that

finally

opened you

I COWER

As is the case with Us,
I make, and You break asunder
whatever comfort I had constructed.
Never certain
what You want from Me;
believing all I am told
about how it is that
Life is supposed to be our unfolding joy,

I cower sometimes,
God,

in the corner, like an animal
who doesn't understand the thunder,
who doesn't understand the lightning—

who doesn't understand
Enlightening.

EVERY BEAUTIFUL SILK

I imagined that God had finally decided

This Cloth

was simply not elegant enough;

had become too ragged,

worn

from so many bouts

of believing in

everything but

The Honeylight

in

the center

But today

God reminded me again

that *every beautiful silk* begins

in the cocoon, where Darkness

is spun into

softer and softer gods

THIS LONGING

Do not pretend that This Longing
has not also lived in you,
swinging, like a pendulum.
You *have* been lost,
and thieved like a criminal,
your Heart
into the darkness.
But life is saddened, Deep Friend,
by going on
without You.
It is like the hand of the mother
who has lost the child.
And if you are anything like me, you have been afraid.
And if you are anything like me,
you have known your own courage.
There is room in this boat:
take your seat.
Take up your paddle, and all of us
—All of Us—
shall row our hearts
back
Home.

IT STILL COMES CLOSE

God is so complex and so simple.
It waits for me to make the first move,
responding only when I extend
a thought,
a word,
a hand,

in Love.

Even as I write I can feel It observing,
very much like a creature
who adores its master,
always curious
what the master will
do next . . .

This is how I know that God is a loving god:

No matter what I do, or have or haven't yet done

It still comes close—

would never
think
to
run

LIGHTBABIES

We are Lightbabies.

Golden Grace.

Wings meant for flight.

We are delicate, and pregnant

with goodness.

We are each made of such a quiet

that the entire Universe

can hear us.

There is only the Opening; the Unfolding

ever happening.

All else are thoughts—

lollipops for the mind.

We are Lightbabies,

parading

as Humankind . . .

LET LIFE

Let life.

It wanted me to tell you that.

Pretend that you've never before heard an ocean's wave.

Or bird's song. Or knew the fragrance of a flower.

Let life in.

Let it appear in your heart like a child

who challenges each of your territories.

Pretend that you have never heard of being left,

of being stifled, or contained.

Let life in again.

And this time

let

it

remain.

O

I don't know how else to tell you, Dear One,
the same,
very same thing
I have said to you
this many millennia

but I shall say it again:

You await *yourself*.
Not me, but *you*.

If you have ever seen a sunflower
turn to follow the sun
then you will remember

the exquisite paradox that

We have together

Destined

And

Designed

O

THIS SUN

There is quiet where the heart breaks.

Even appealing to God for love is
a step outside the sacred ground,
and a noise that breaks the Silence.

I always knew that Love would find me,
but I didn't dream that this was how:

A Brightening, happening from a place *within*,
illumining every darkness.

Life is loyal and patient, and
eternally has it watched me grow . . .

ever toward *this* sun.

LAY THE HAMMER DOWN

God says, "*Lay the hammer down.*"
Which is really my own voice, make no mistake.
And it is *your* own voice, too.
So, "Lay the hammer down"
and put your hand to your lips,
or lay it against your heart, whispering
"Sweet forgiveness,"
though there is nothing to forgive.
All we do is try to love.
It appears as everything: anger, fear, and
hurt of every kind.

But all we do is try to love.

There is nothing to forgive
save
lifting The Hammer again . . .

IT IS YOUR SEASON

It is your season.
Though every one of your
leaves has fallen, and new growth has not yet come,
it is your season.
Though your roots are the only proof you have
that you are still among the living;
though
leaves, nay fruit, seem but
a far-off dream—

it is your season.

Do you know how I know
that this is so?
Because the Beloved loves to play
with Becoming, turning "Patience"
over Its tongue just before
It
finally
whispers

"Blooooom!"

ALL THINGS THAT
HAVE FALLEN AWAY

You can trust the process.
*Life knows what
It is doing.*
All things that have fallen away

leave ribbons,
on signposts,
guiding you
to the

heart

of

this

moment

It is from the bottom of
this Light-well
that we rise to greet
the next moment:

It's just a breath

SOUL LANGUAGE

Speak in a Soul Language
so that Everyone can hear.
Unwind This Story of Humanity
with a
presence so precious,
even God cannot give it definition.
Practice loving so deeply
that the word for tears
becomes
"ocean"
and
the School of Compassion
is the
World's Greatest Institution.
Let no one walk alone
on this journey that is
Ours
to share:
Speak in a Soul Language,
so that Everyone can hear.

HEARTBODY THE BALM

Sometimes Awakening
is a bruise on
the
Heartbody.
I wonder if all of the
tender creatures
made of wings
thin carapaces
veins of light
petal-skins
the ones made *fragile* and *fragrant* for the world
can
withstand
such
ongoing
storms?
Sometimes Awakening
is a bruise on the Heartbody—
but the Heartbody *the balm*
for Awakening.

THE BEST DANCERS

Maybe God keeps me here like this
to stumble a little.
If I were to suddenly just
turn into light,
blinding *myself* even
to the most precious and necessary illusions,
then what hand could hold my own?
Where would rest a weary head?
What good use for warm hearts;
for hot tears?
Why eyes to see?
Why arms to open?
Which Lovefamily to fall into?

The Best Dancers know
what grace

every
stumble
contains

LOVE ITSELF

Please do not regret
all those moments that have brought you
Here.
If you are reading this,
then your perseverance has been answered,
and a Grace is coming.
So for now, hold on loosely to where you are.
And like knots on a rope that mark your reaching,
hand over hand
you will continue to climb—
sometimes through ecstasy,
sometimes through white agony, but
higher
into ever more light.
This same formula over and over again,
until that day you find yourself
just a beacon. Only flame.
In a place
where even Love Itself
has come undone.

BE RECEIVED

Move slowly from these old skins.
Your belly is raw, your back is tender—
you are rudimentary now.

Move softly from these old skins.
Let the full bodyweight
of all your innocence
down.

Be received.
Be received by the broad earth of your worthiness.
Cast off everything
everyone else has known for you.

Move gratefully from these old skins.
And this time, if you toughen,
decide

for whom?

NEVER BROKEN

I am my own Home now.

Wherever I move,

the Light

moves with me.

I open all of the windows and the doors

so that God can come and go, easily.

I don't know why God takes such delight

in this House I call "Me".

This place

where hearts come

to be broken.

At the end of the Long Day I always ask,

"God? *Why*, hearts to be broken?"

And God always replies,

"Never broken, *dear Lover*—

only *Opened*."

ONE STEP AT A TIME

And the mind said, "How will I handle all of it?"

Then, before the mind could answer,
something akin to a whisper
—a presence with a Lover's touch—
stirred within me,
saying:

"One step at a time."

A great way opened up just then,

and through the air, each foot rose and fell;
each sole met and kissed
the stones

One Step at a Time

the Now, a lover,

Her
body

draped

just

so

O

You leave me because you leave me,
but I have never gone anywhere.

I am always home,
setting lanterns
in the window
for you.

Look into my divine eye, Dear One—
do you not always see yourself there?

One day you will tire
of telling yourself
that you cannot
look into my eyes
because you have
"failed" me
"again".

You will hear the mind
but you will no longer
engage it.

And you will surrender to the kiss,
and never again play the desperate lover,
turning your back to me,

Pretending

To

Be

Asleep

O

SILENCE AGAIN

The Mind will Think, and Image and Vision
because that is the job it was given.
When you've finally, exhaustedly,
tried everything else,
try *Silence*.
The kind that is found within the loudest noise.

Speak Silence so sweetly that the body,
with all its rumblings and pains,
and the Mind, with all of its ghouls and gains,
buys in—

Silence, Silence, Silence

and

Silence

again

OPENING WHAT HAS BEEN CLOSED

Opening what has been Closed,

letting Light in,
you stir, move again,
keening, arching, dying
to the warmth.

So many times
(my God, so many)

Triumphs

within each of your darknesses . . .

Opening what has been Closed,

letting

Light

in

WHILE YOU WERE OUT

While You were out,
many things transpired.
A sky was born.
Love & Laughter married.
Ten thousand suns were birthed.
I awoke a Butterfly,
my wings burst into song,
and I even changed my name

while You were out.

Planets began to dance,
and all colors traded hues.
Stars turned themselves into ocean bottoms;
grasshoppers into gazelles,
and I left the earth
and returned

Courageous

All
while You were out.

THE SOUL KEEPS INVITING

There is that knowing-moment
when you realize: *Something has ended.*
You round a corner, taking a casual left
or a sharp right, and suddenly you just know

that something, somewhere has
already turned to ash.

Then your heart begins to harden;
all of your actions, informed by a decision,
to do everything you can to stop yourself

from loving what's left.

Photo frame by bauble, you begin
to practice imagining them gone.
You try to picture all of the pictures
without faces—just frames—
packed away, or still set in the slim
film of plastic before you slid a fine
fingernail into them:

frames of your Dreams . . .

Now the cat curls wherever you curl
because it knows, too, that something
is preparing itself

to steal off into the woods, and to lie down
beneath the canopy of stars or clouds;
the branches, and the boughs;
the needles, and the leaves;
around the roots of a thing . . .

One million diamonds will tumble
from your eyes, made from a different
kind of pressure: *the force of the Soul.*

Oh, the staggering gift of growth
and everything, *everything*

the soul keeps inviting you to grow *into.*

IF EVER THESE WORDS

If ever these words
do not sit well
at your heart's
table

You can always
invite them to
leave

and they will
go *so*
peacefully . . .

Instead, You and God
might sit together
at *your own* Heart-table.
In the candlelight.
And the quiet.
And create:

new Heartwords
no one has ever before heard!

God wants nothing more than to

be

Your

Heartscribe

PRECIOUS OCCURRENCE

I am a precious occurrence,
and I don't have long.
We are a precious occurrence.
And as long as we think we have,
we don't have long.
Too much time is being spent
running
from face to face
asking, "What is my name?"

If you don't yet know it,
or if you've forgotten,
then become still, go within
and answer it.

You are a Precious Occurrence:
Tell *Us* your name.

IN EVERYTHING

I don't know what all the other poets are writing about.
All I know is that this morning
I rose and have been searching
everywhere now, for inspiration.

I don't know if most poets wake
and peer first into the teakettle,
then, the bottom of the cup;
search the corners of the kitchen
or out the kitchen window, or if they
stare blankly into a white screen,
or down at their pad of paper, pen in hand,
hand hovering then listing . . .

Maybe other poets rise radiant, but I know
that today I rise and am surprised
at a face that changes: yesterday
The Lover, the day before, Youth;
today, a face of putty; malleable; too much of it.

But maybe this is okay. Maybe this is just the kind of god
God hoped would come, and would be courageous,
looking for Itself—

finding Itself Nowhere, and in Nothing,
and finding Itself

in Everything.

UNRELENTING GRACE

Life conspires to bless us with an
unrelenting Grace.
Who among us has not been touched
by this generous hand,
freeing us,
one
or many layers
at a time?
You are the lucky one
who has known annihilation
and then absorption
back into the Love
you seek.
And it is *you* who knows
that even as the soul-cry rends your very chest,
the whole of the Universe
shakes
with Love.
In this place of All
there is at long, long last

no place
left
to
fall.

WHAT IS IT THAT YOU WERE GIVEN?

What is it that you were given?

I mean from the loss.

After, what was taken.

That very thing you could never live without.

The person or place;

the secret, or circumstance—

now that it is gone,

or has been found out,

and you can no longer call *it* foundation

what is it that you were given?

You know, and I know, this:

there is a hollowing out.

Something comes and opens you up

right

down

the

middle

and from that moment on

you are no longer immune to this world.

You wake, you wander,
every familiar, now a foreign.
You walk as through water
until you make it back to your bed
and finally, even there—
your sheets; your own pillow's scent different,
as if daily someone repaints your room,
displaces something,
disturbs a cherished memento.

You see,
sometimes we *are* emptied.
We are emptied
because
Life wants us to know

so

much

more

Light.

O

Light
is your true nature.
You can be no other.
You exist outside of mind,
yet inside the universal womb.

Leave the mind behind
until you are so sure you are the sun
that you name yourself an

eternal

rising

dawn

O

TILTED LADDERS

Who knew
that the girl who climbed trees
and ran through summers, barefoot

who picked berries from atop ladders
set against thick, thorny vines,
and blossoms

would so many years later
find herself

still climbing

tilted ladders
set against thick,
thorny vines
determined
to find
The Fruit

before
Summer's
end.

MY NAME

"God is shy," they often say, and
"God will come, and go away,"
but sleep I did, until I woke,
The Night—its darkness finally broke—
and everything I dreamed upon, it came.

God appeared and sang out, "Love!"

Oh, *God appeared and called me by My Name.*

SO MUCH LOVING

The spaces in between *are your home.*

One day soon,

you will become so good at

Silence

that everything in you will

Sing!

So good at Spaciousness,

that opening even one eye, or smiling,

will be more joy than you can stand!

So good at Freedom,

that being bound in the body

will seem a small price to pay

for all of the Light-tricks

you've learned to play.

Oh, Dear One, without this Grand Adventure,

so much Loving

never

would

have

happened

KNOW YOUR SELF AS LIGHT

Know Your Self as Light.
Bigger even than Breath.
Larger even than the Whole.
Quieter even than the Quiet that holds You.

Know Your Self as Held.
Softer even than as before;
Deeper even than any Darkness.

When the Lightbody of You
breathes without borders,
knows not
even of the concept,
or of any bounds at all . . .

when you Know Your Self
as only Light,
summoning the Mystery
to move through You—

exquisite, innocent instrument
of the long
long, eternity of song—

then

Know Your Self as
Life's greatest Laughter;
Life's greatest Lover,
beckoning the Mystery

come hither.

THE RIGHT KIND OF PARENT

God, you are the right kind of Parent.
You know just when to shelter,
when to hold,
and
when to open your hands
and whisper,

"Fly"

EVERYWHERE, HEART

Heart is hiding everywhere,
and when I look
without eyes
I fall
immediately
into
that warm abyss.
And then
the concepts
that were my crutch,
the judgments
that were my prison,
the armor
that was my skin,
disappears

and

the heart
hides nowhere,
the seeker
ceases seeking,

knowing everywhere,

Everywhere, Heart.

ALL BELOVEDS

You are shyer than I imagined, God.
Now I have been given the understanding
that it is You who waits for the caress.
It is You who yearns to know Me,
and to witness
Our Love, loving.

What I understand anew is this:

As I run toward You, *You run toward Me . . .*

But isn't this how

All Beloveds

reunite?

NOW IS YOUR TIME

Now is your time—*no more excuses.*

What are those wings for, anyway?

When you wake, do not first move outside,
but stoke the flames *within* that wait
for the breath of your
Self Divinity

Then let that Fire Roar

fanned
by
Each of Your
fledgling

F
l
i
g
h
t
s

A GRADUATE

Lay me down in Love.
Anoint my thoughts in such a way
that Heaven's supply of Lovebreath
will almost run out today.

Bless my knees with Love.
Ready them for all those times ahead.
In me you have found a Love Soldier,
and one more loyal to This Cause than any.

As many ways as there are to Love,
let me know them then.
Let's decide, God,
that I am *already*

a

Graduate.

WHEN DID YOU STOP SINGING?

This morning God asked me,
"When did you stop singing?"

At first, I was angered.
Then, I let the question be.

"Why," said I,
"I believe it was when I began to follow
every thought that was given to me
by my parents,
and then by my peers,
and then by any passing stranger.
I believe it was the moment I began to choose
achievement over Alchemy
and competition over Compassion.
It was that morning I rose,
and put my feet into shoes
too tight for Freedom;
when I listened, instead of Music,
to mankind."

"I believe," said I, "that I stopped singing
the moment I stopped hearing Birdsong
or laughed with the sounds of Laughter."

"And when did you stop dancing?" said God.
"Or being enchanted by stories?
Or stop finding comfort in the sweet territory
of silence?"

"Why," answered I, "It was, you see, when I forgot that

I

am

You."

GO OUTSIDE AND PLAY

"Go outside and play!"

said God.

"I have given you Universes as fields to run free in!

And here—take this and wrap yourself in it—

It's called *LOVE*,

and it will always, *always* keep you warm.

And stars! The sun and the moon and the stars!

Look upon these often, for they will remind you of your

own light!

And eyes . . . oh, gaze into *every* Lover's eyes,

gaze into every Other's eyes,

for they have given you *their* Universes

as fields to run free in.

There.

I have given you everything you need.

Now go, go, *go outside* and PLAY!"

YOU WERE MEANT

All of This:
it is preparation for walking in the world
as Light.
You have been found now,
and the running of many lifetimes
is over.
So as each layer of dust
is wiped clean from the surface
the You
you have known
must disperse.

Let *this* Light become
your Speech & your Silence.

Let the grief
that has lived you,
pass away.

Let the people
who love You,
Love Themselves.

Let the Earth shake,
the Stars burn
the Skies break
when You do:

as painful as this part is,

You were meant to know your Light.

O

I am the map
that guides you through
all of the territories of fear
that you create.

Yet the most useful tool
is
Love,
and the least useful
Is the mind.

The mind is a cap that is meant to be worn very lightly.

What is it that happens when you graduate,
or win the big game?

You throw your cap high into the air
and don't even worry about

trying

to

recover

It

O

READY

You never really know
when it will come.

Rising, laying foot
into the same imprint
you've made
yesterday
and the day before
and yes,
eternally before.

But some time
that superbly hairline crack
in your well-preserved casing
will suffer *a Grace*.

You can call it crisis, or crumble,
or, you can see it
as the first time your Truth
has succeeded in escaping,

like the soft and persistent
pressings of a chick

ready to leave the egg,

ready to *know* Life

for the first time.

BEAUTIFUL DREAMER

Beautiful Dreamer—
Who Are You,
sitting in the seat of this soul?
Bless your innocent eyes,
half closed.
Bless your tender jaw,
still set in confusion.
Bless your full, beating heart,
so kissed with Light.

Bless the hand that writes,
and the breath that hesitates,
and the World that waits

for You.

DIVINE SILENCES

I wait for the time, God,

when we shall greet

each other

in the reflection

of

every water into which I gaze.

For now

I keep my faith in

Us

by honoring

every one of

Our

Divine

Silences

TO LOVE YOURSELF

To Love yourself, start here:

take your own hand—put it to your lips

then

lay the soft of your cheek to the round of your shoulder

where

the faint musk

of the enduring dreams and the labors of your life

perfume you.

It's a start.

It's a beginning.

Now the ache of your heart

has

a

surface

THREE DOGS KNOWING

They don't set out to do anything grand.

They play, the three of them:
Black and Burr-ridden,
Speckled and Bright-eyed,
Sleek and Questioning.
Every morning the play continues,
tugging one another this way and that
along throughout a day.

If He sits, scratching and gazing out across
the great divide of valleys,
She will bring Him an enduring piece of hat
or garden hose or
the last fourth of a plastic ball
and drop it at His feet.

If the One with the moon-colored eyes
lies in the ivy, with sun on Her ribs
and leaves in Her ears
the other two will attack mid-dream
with nip and tug at
neck and tail.

It is pure genius and heart.

Three dogs living out the Mystery
every moment,

while it slips like water

through all of *my grasping.*

SO QUIETLY

I try always to remember what
Stillness is—

why the soul of This Being needs it.

But there is society, you know,
and there are responsibilities . . .

I walk in the Outer World and forget,
then walk in the Inner world and remember,
that everything—
every thought form, every dream,
every feathered creature's wing—
was birthed
in
a
profound

Stillness.

This morning I don't think I've seen anything more
beautiful
than the birds, silhouetted by the steam rising from the
rooftop,
the steam, silhouetted by the rising pines behind,
and the entire scene

so

quietly

Divine

SHINE

God says for me to tell you this:

Nothing needs fixing;

everything desires

a

Celebration.

You were made to bend

so that you would find

all of the many miracles at your feet.

You were made to stretch

so that you could discover

your own beautiful face of Heaven

just above

all that you think you must shoulder.

When I appeal to God to speak to me,

I'm feeling just as small and alone as you might be.

But this is when, for no particular reason at all,

I begin to

shine

RISE TOGETHER

It's a beautiful time to be alive.

And the long walk home is peopled—

We are *everywhere.*

Yet the struggle to *surrender*

is where we often walk alone.

So the next time you fall,

look

to either side where you lie

and take the hand

of your dear Brother or Sister

whose own clothes are muddied.

We can rise together,

even if we fall alone.

For it's a beautiful time to be alive,

even

on this

long

walk

home

WE JUST WANT LOVE

Everything
you thought you wanted—

so did I.

As it turns out,
funny,
we just want love.

Aspirations and lofty notions call—
funny,
we just need love.

Knowing you very little
I feel as if I know you well:

the moan beneath the chest,
the pleading in the eyes:
one giant asking
in a yet unformed question.

One answer surely,
in many forms will come.
And I will say its name.
And I will call it:

Love.

UNREASONABLY

"Show yourself to me," said I to God again.

And this is what happened next:

I became pregnant with Light.
My eyes were sunrise and sunset, both.
Freckles announced themselves planets and stars,
and beamed upon my cheeks.
Each of my lips became a kiss to the other,
my ears heard oceans of life.
Between my eyes there was an indigo wheel,
between my toes, blond fields.
My hands remembered climbing-trees,
my hair, each lover's fingers.

And then I whispered,
"But why have you made me this *way?"*
And it was told to me this:

"Because I have never had Your name before,
nor heard the way You sing it.
Nor stared into the universe through eyes like These.
Nor laughed This way, nor felt the path that
These tears take.

Because I have not known These ecstasies,
nor risen to These heights, nor experienced
every nuance of the innocence
with which You create Your lows.

Nor how a Heart could grow so wide,
or break so easily,
or Love

quite *so unreasonably."*

NOT YOUR SONG

That is enough for now.

Fall silent Dear One,

for *this, is not* Your song.

Turn your eyes inward and let your mouth remain
closed;
your tongue soft and quiet
until you are sure,
quite sure,
that you are done.

Then,

re-string Your instrument, Dear One.

PUPPIES

I am simply dreaming a way

to love everyone within

arm's reach.

I have help:

you come toward me

with an aching in your eyes,

and a sadness leftover in your smiles.

In this new dream I am dreaming for me,

I include all of you.

Do you want to know what *my* love is?

It is *your* love.

And all of us

Puppies

curling into

one

warm

heap

O

You have become accustomed to living
under such heavy robes,
Beloveds.

But the way to lighten this mortal load
is to spin me like straw
into
gold.

Sit down in the dark room of your inner plane,
where the sun is brighter than
the sun
and become an alchemist.
But first—
say all of those words to me
that fill your heart;
that cry your song,
then
you will be ready

for
our
silent
banquet

O

THIS I KNOW

Close your eyes.

There is another kiss coming.

Can you catch the perfume of

The Divine?

Can you hear That voice,

soft and low?

There is another kiss coming,

this

I

Know

DEEP INSIDE

Deep inside
in the quietest depth
Nothing
is
speaking
or
saying
a word.

But The Silence I seek,
yet choose to run from,

is the voice of
God, *unheard.*

THE SWEET UNVEILING

The sweet Unveiling is so becoming

there is perhaps nothing

more beautiful.

The *glide* that you once called

"walking".

Your fears

dropped as gently as lingerie.

As Who You Are,

naked child,

turns every purpose

Lightward—

toward what has always been

right

here

shining

as

You.

BY GOODNESS

Create something *good*.
Never take a photo without something heart-shaped
somewhere in it.
Don't paint anything without placing somewhere
a circle, or a spiral.
Try not to write any story that doesn't give
to the world
one
virtuous character
whom we can Love.

Sand and make smooth the edges of every object
in your life . . .

There are too many of us
who need to see something
heart-shaped
or rounded, or spiraled
or smoothed or
worn

by

goodness

over

time

THE HEART CAN ALWAYS SEE

The Inner eye is the only True

"I"

The Heart can always see

where
Loss and Gain
meet

Being turned inside-out is not so bad—
this is how we learn
what the body
really is.

Then,

how to live

as

The Heart

on

The Sleeve

ONE MORE BIRD

I guess God chose me

as one more bird

who sings about

Cages

and how

they were never

meant to arrest

Songs

or

Wings,

but were only meant to

awaken

in *every caged Bird*

the Longing

to fly.

WILLINGNESS

We can become lighter & lighter.

We can pull from the soundless sound.

We can sit completely still in movement.

We can open every cell, as wide as it can open.

How, you say? And I say,

by Willingness first.

Then faith in the Unbelievable.

By Perseverance beyond your idea of it,

then by layer upon layer of Patience.

Now, Grace moves through, unannounced.

Now, the Unimaginable. Miracles.

Then Darkness. The Womb. Gestation.

Birth. Then Light.

Then Willingness again . . .

LOOSE

There is a new perch, and a nest.

There are endings ending and beginnings
not yet standing.

A new home; I am thirty-five.
Vistas, vantage points all changed.

Old questions still rumble
yet new answers
move into me

in globes of light.

What interests me most?
Awakening.
Losing my *self* in Love.
Telling a new story, and finally
no story at all.

Then, becoming sunlight

loose

in the fields of my life.

MAKE AND MEND

From Stillness
I reach my hand and
touch the face of God.
Both fulfilled and unrequited,
my heart feels
Whole and yet Divided.
Out beyond and deep within
exists this "I".

Yet on
earth I make and mend
such *mortal* wings
with which to
try to fly.

KISS THIS SUN

The Human weight is heavy
when you focus on It
instead
of
Silence
&
Light

But these words won't make
any sense at all
until you try it.

It becomes a long, cold day
when we leave the Home,
moving out into the world,
without
first pausing to

kiss

This

sun

O

Conceive of an unfolding
and I will become
a blanket made
of heavenlight;

a place of shelter
where you may come to rest
and to be comforted
by the greatness
of my love
for you.

You see that we conjoin quicker
than thought can ever be produced:
a turning inside-out
of every shàdow.

But how can you hear divine answers
or pose eternal questions
when your mind is still so full

of the

Noise of The Ages?

O

TO MAKE LOVE

Everything was meant to fit together;
to stay close;
to make love.

We were created to give ourselves to every love that
visits—

like *flower* awaits *bee,*
entering
each
of its

tender invitations . . .

All beings were meant to fit together.

To stay close.

To make love.

WE ARE AWAKENING ONE ANOTHER

We are awakening one another.
It does not matter whose heart
still clings to the vine.

In time

everyone will know

that

each

passing

moment

contains the changing seasons.

That what we cling to as seed
we must let go of to grow.
Must champion to take root.
Must fall in love with as tender shoot.

Spring, summer, winter, fall

this is *All* . . .

yet hearts do cling.

They do.

IF WE ARE NAKED

We say that we will have a Good Life.
This is a guarantee
if we are kind to one another.
If we are patient.
If when I speak, you listen
and if when you speak, I hear you.
This is assured,
if we continue to look for one another.
If we want to find.
If when I am here, I am seen,
and if when you are here, I see you.
We say that this will be a Good Life.
This is a guarantee
if We are naked with one another.
If We are clotheless.
If, when I am vulnerable,
you shelter,
and if, when you are defenseless,

I protect.

THE ONE WE DO

That's what It does, you know—Love.

It stands between people,
connecting their hearts
with Divinity,

then

when we open our mouths to speak,
it turns a language we haven't
fully remembered

into

The One We Do

PRIMARY COLORS

"God?" said I,

"How do I walk in this world and
love the walking in it?"

And God said to me,

"I have given you your Smile.
Practiced genuinely, a smile alone
will heal you, and all the world.

"I have given you Tears: they are the Soul's language.
Cleanse yourself daily with these, in Joy or in Grief,
and you will heal yourself and all the world.

"I have given you my Heart. Become intimate with it.
Then, you will make love with yourself, and all the
world.

"And I have given you Laughter, the universal language.
If you speak it often, it can heal you and all the world.

"When these are the primary colors on your palette,
You will never again need words from me—

nay, Beloved,
You will not even need to use
your own anymore . . . ."

HOW THE SOUL

Before you enter the world today,
be sure to visit the edges
of this great Light-tapestry,
and then the universes beyond.

We have each been given the job
of staying True,
and the Soul can only go so long
without a drink from

your

Well of *Light.*

This is how we endure
the walk of the human, Being.

Oh, Humane Being
sustained
by
Love,

how the Soul joys
in wearing your hands
to caress the human experience

face by face, time by time,
in this dense duality

Sorrowful and Sublime

THE BELOVED'S STORMS

Clouds were meant to occasionally
cover the sun
but I notice how
The Beloved's storms love to
ravish the sky

leaving

Our entire body

naked as a moonbeam

LIGHT

Lightearth, Lightskies

Lightwords, Lighteyes

Light weaved, Light filled, Light dreamed, *Light.*

Light when the Sun wakes, Light when the Moon

wakes, Light when the Heart wakes, *Light.*

Light in the Dreamnight, Light in the Heavensight,

Light in the Heartbright, *Light.*

Lightwarm, Lightday, Lightform, Lightplay,

Lightsing, Lightsong, *Light.*

Light in the dim sight, Light in the dark night,

Light   Light   Light

I AM THAT I AM

I AM THAT I AM

and

so much more:

the light, the sound;

the living of Love on the ground.

I could show you every feather in the wing.

Every color and hue.

Only beautiful things...

but

I AM THAT I AM

wants to

love

whatever has not yet known it.

Whomever has not yet felt it.

However life's not yet done it.

There is still so much loving,

yet to be found,

just

living God on the ground.

A BEAUTIFUL NAME

Give yourself a beautiful name.

You

are

light

playing the human game.

Brighten each word

and

flame your heart—

didn't you know?

You

are

God's

art!

O

You see, each time you visit the heart
its kiss opens a little wider
and all of the light
that lives there
is free
to seek its natural place
in the order of things.

And even though the eyes seem
as if they sit in the saddle of the mind,
they are only eyes,
and it is only the mind.

There is a higher "I" you know,
and it is me,

watching over you always, and

reveling

in

your

Light

display

O

MOMENTS OF GOLD

I love when Light makes that sound.
It comes, sometimes, as if from the edges
of the room:

a

volume

of sunlight

This soft buzzing, quickening in soundless sound—
like there is honey being made, everywhere,

everywhere

moments

of

Gold

CLOSER TO THE SUN

Where God and I meet
Where the Beloved and I meet
Is where the whisper meets the ear
Is where the moonbeam meets the water
Is where The Dewdrop & The Bud

tell stories
spin fables

about which one of them is actually

closer

to

the

Sun

A LIVING PLACE

Sun breaks open in my heart
without moderation.
There is *heaven* here.
But don't ask me to come Home just yet—
don't try to summon all of this love Home,
for I have only just found
a Living Place.
Somewhere I can put my love.

A grassy field, where on my back I lie,
musing at the broad sky, knowing *I* can light it.
Why, even the stars disappear
in the making of *this* kind of love.

Oh, there are too many ways to say the same thing.
But this is why God likes to rest at my feet—

to hear
what Love will say
next

THIS KISS

It's all right, God, that we court like this:

as perfectly planned as

Fireflies & Twilight

at the blended edge of summer's night.

By the time I turn to look at you

from beneath this blushing skin,

you have already sent an angel's breath

from some *new* heaven within.

Oh, Beloved within me, I *do love* Thee—

yet, it is *to Me* I whisper! And to The All of Life that

gathers in That name.

Oh, it is *this kiss*

I

bid

Divinity

claim.

THINGS WILL BE DIFFERENT NOW

Things will be different now, you know.

Not the snows, blanketing mountains in June.

Not, "The frost came early" or "stayed late".

The kind of different

that stains the soul.

That leaves an Innocent dusted

with

every new color of God.

Once you have seen deeply

and been deeply seen

you know that

nothing

has ever, ever been as it seemed.

That your own reflection is

every Christ, every Goddess, every Buddha, and Brahmin—

put simply: the *Everyone's Heart.*

BODY OF GOD

Today I awakened quieter than God
and stretched my Self toward the sky
to caress the celestial bodies

with

the

Body of God

All night long
The Sun awaited my eyes.
And now that they are upon Her
She rises, as Divined as every Siren, every Muse
every
Body of God.

Even Ocean sways and rocks
in gentle wait for me to wake—

even Moon

even Sky

even Silence

Even Silence awaits the awakening of my voice
to tenderly kiss Its body of sounds

still

in

the

Body

of

God

WHY RUN?

The worst that can happen is that you find
Yourself in The Center,
where there is only Silence.

Nothing comes and goes.
Nothing is your name.

Yet

Something is around you.
Something cloaks you.

It is Goodness.

The worst that can happen is this.

So why run?

Why run from
The Gentle Darkness?
The Quiet Sun?

LIKE WE ARE

Before I even conjure it
You answer.
I try to say 'I Love You'
and my own face
—wonder of wonders—
appears before
my Heart.

So I wait for the dawn.
Thinking that if I lie
still as a baby bird
curled in the egg
You
will come,
ushered by The Calling,
out from the face of the deep,
where darkness & dawning
are still deciding

like We are

where One begins and the Other ends.

I have told you: *become still*.
I have told you: *taste the darkness*.
I have told you: *see this light*.
I have told you: *patience*.
I have told you: *will*.
I have told you:

Love.

And I have shown you this:

Pockets full of diamonds
Stardust throughout
Moonbeams in between

And

Love.

I have placed you here to love.
There are countless ways to do this . . .

Pick up your instrument
your pen
your paintbrush
your voice
and

make me real

to
the
world

O

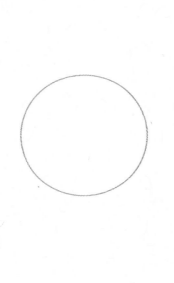

Em Claire was born and raised in the Pacific Northwest of the United States. She invites people everywhere to travel a path which honors all life-affirming belief systems, emphasizes inclusiveness, focuses on living in harmony with all of life, and seeks to demonstrate that love is the most powerful force in the universe. She may be reached at *www.emclairepoet.com* and *www.Lovism.com*.

You are invited to read the Afterword of *Home Remembers Me* over on my website. I have chosen to publish the Afterword there in order to allow the book to remain "quiet" and to stay within the pale of the poetic and the lyrical, which can often create a more right-brained experience and take us to a place where deep healing has been known to occur.

When you are ready, know that the Afterword contains many offerings on ways to more skillfully move through challenging times. These many sources for support are ready and available to you and will be updated often at:

www.emclairepoet.com

O

I am helped by *Margaret Emerson's* articulations of both *medicine walks*, and *vision quests* in my descriptions found in the Introduction. I thank her for allowing me to offer by extension a basic and general representation of these ancient, beautiful and sacred practices. For additional and more extensive reading on these traditions which many different tribes native to the Americas have in common, you are invited to visit my website. (*Contemplative Hiking Along the Colorado Front Range* by Margaret Emerson © 2010 Reprinted with permission.)

The poem "When Did You Stop Singing?" was inspired by a quote from Gabrielle Roth in her book *Maps to Ecstasy.* She graciously gave me permission to include that poem here. Bless you, Gabrielle, and thank you for the healing you brought and will continue to bring to so many through Dance. (Gabrielle Roth February 4, 1941 – October 22, 2012 • *Maps to Ecstasy* By Gabrielle Roth © 1998 Reprinted with permission of New World Library, Novato CA. *www. newworldlibrary.com)*